Grandma's
Prayer
Book
GLORIA GRAHAM
AF372892

NEWMAN SPRINGS PUBLISHING
320 Broad Street
Red Bank, NJ 07701

First originally published by Newman Springs Publishing 2024

ISBN 979-8-89061-355-4 (Paperback)
ISBN 979-8-89061-356-1 (Digital)

Printed in the United States of America

To Victoria, Doretha, Bettye and Kate—

My grandchildren-----whose memories I cherish more than life, are truly a gift from God. They are always close to my heart and I could not be more proud of them. Whenever they were sick, I felt helpless and would pray even harder for them to get well soon. I would give anything for them and I am so grateful to have them in my life. They inspire me to do more and become more.

GRANDMA'S PRAYERS BOOK

A grandma always looked after all of the grandchildren, great-grandchildren, daughters, and sons. I am a mother who cares about what happens on the streets and how our children die every day, where reparations are set forth. We hear about building up, but who saves the children?

I am asking God to help us challenge our fears. I am set to hold their heads on my shoulder and around my breasts. I began to pray.

Let me be whole for a long little while until I reached my desire. How can we forget while waiting longer? Fix me, Lord. The streets are not safe. Are we turning back to slavery? My God, thank you for watching over me.

Think about the children of Israel, who could depend on Jehovah to forgive. I desire to reach a goal. There is a lot of sickness in the world that makes me whole for a little while on this earth—my children.

Please make reparations; I am still their goodness. Lend me, O God, your strength. Hallelujah! O Lord, give me the strength to make it through as a grandmother. Here are my weeping prayers.

The work of the spirit comes from faithfully blessing the truth. Reparations are the sons, not conflict and accountability. My Jesus Heavenly Communion miracle of healing endorsed power over the elements.

People come to church for help, and there is a known tendency to help back in return, where reparations are preached as helping people. Our neighbor needs help with the killing in the street. Mothers bring their children and grandchildren for help, so what is the need? My God, the Lord, is my life. Who should be the shame of the church's reparations? How can I live seeing my grandmother in pain? I remember her. My granddaughter says life is kind of hard sometimes. I am pretty sure you know that I am learning to be alone and do this on my own with God's help first, as Granny taught me to know who God is and where I stand in him as I follow Granny's footsteps. Amen.

Discussion
What are reparations?
Preaching
Lift in God's Spirit

RESURRECTION

Happy Resurrection! Jesus had an assignment given to him by God. Jesus cried out, "Why did you forsake me, God?" Jesus picked up the cross and started carrying it.

You are not alone in your sins, but Jesus stated, "My God! My God!" Jesus cried out again, "Why! My father had a command. I am 100 percent man and 100 percent God!" while being nailed to the cross for the sins he had not done. Amen! Gloria! Happy Easter.

Discussion
John 11:25–26
What is resurrection?

 WHAT IS FAITH

The living faith of God hears our prayer, Lord.

Jesus will fight your battles, and God will not forsake us.

Here, two Tennessee young men were expelled, just like two of your disciples, for speaking out the truth and for freedom. We have received not the spirit of the world, but the spirit of Jesus and God, yes! We are walking and weeping through the darkest valley. Who am I? God's grace? Amen.

Discussion
Hebrews 11:1
What is grace?
What are Christian faiths?

SPEAK, LORD

The Lord is speaking. "Peace be still over the water. Let me take your hands and lead you to the cross, for the water is still."

Whatever your desire, God, I will be humble. Help me, Lord, find life. Elijah, can you hear the sound of Jesus's voice and the heaven's rain coming down?

Be still in the spirit, for the Lord is speaking. Amen.

Discussion
Psalm 85:8

HOLY THY GOD

Holy is thy God. Open your eyes to the spirit of God. What shall you do? It is not your eyes but God's. He spoke to you. Jesus will take you out of the darkness and bring you to the light of God. "Follow me because I have a job for you on this earth." Answer that. God gifts you by faith, but who wants to come to the light of the eyes of God? He creates heaven and earth and holds on a little while longer. Amen.

Discussion
Leviticus 20:26
What is the spirit of God?

THE TRUTH I AM STANDING

Truth! I am standing. I will overcome it one day. O God of mercy! Mercy is when God gives us goodness and grace. Mercy is when Jesus came down and spared us with a blessing. Truly, mercy is God's grace that lives inside each of us. Thanks be to God and his grace and mercy—encouraging us to grow in Christ's light and truth, where I stand. Amen.

Discussion
Ephesians 6:14–15
Encouragement
Confidence in God and desires
Truth
Fighting for justice

JUSTICE OF REPARATIONS

Fight for justice! Let's fight for social justice and keep pushing for freedom. I lift my head, Lord, and cry out, "Why our children?" I am weeping, Lord. We are disbanded in the sin of Tyre Nichols. My Heavenly Father, feed us. Give us social justice, Lord of God. My prayer, affirmation, and gratitude in the spirit! Hallelujah! Amen.

> Discussion
> Isaiah 11:4–9
> Vulnerability of a grandmother
> Holy Spirit of God's grace
> The life under justice system
> Weapons of under justice

GOD'S STRENGTH

It is God's strength and love that give me salvation and open my eyes to the Lord if salvation comes with faith, spirit, and the belief of assurance to trust in his holy name. The space is open. Amen!

Discussion
Unchanging hand

JUSTICE OF GOD

Peace and justice! I think about how Jesus died on the cross for us and how Dr. Martin Luther King Jr. fought for freedom, and there is no freedom or justice here in America for people of color.

Lord, hear my prayer for all. One day, we will come together as one. Amen.

Discussion
Psalm 37: 28
What is the power of justice?

HOLY LAND OF GOD

Oh! Holy God! Holy is the Spirit of God and the freedom of God. Deliver me from evil and transform and restore my soul. Hallelujah, Lord of the Holy Ghost. Gloria.

Open Discussion

TRUST IN GOD, FEAR NOT GOD!

Trust in God. He will lead you to the truth. The Holy Spirit is the truth. Remember whose faith you should follow, and trust in God in his name. When you get to know who God is, fear not, my children, because the Lord is always on your side. Take a breath, step away, and step into God, who loves you. Having fear of God is like knowing within yourself who God is. Amen.

DIVINE FATHER

My divine Father, the light of God, illuminates and brightens. The Spirit of God gives us peace. Amen. Gloria.

Discussion
Divinity
What is the difference between divinity and Jesus?

KINGDOM OF GOD

The kingdom of God gives us delivery in Christ, the Lord, which is set up in my heart. Jesus is in my heart, healing me and making me hold again. Amen. Gloria.

Discussion
Do you know Christ?

WILDERNESS

Preach the Word and praise him—God of the wilderness. We trust in the struggles, the hardships, and the wilderness of God. Amen and YWAH. Gloria.

Discussion
What does it look like in God's eye, and what is fulfillment with hope?
Trust
Struggles
What was God's purpose in the wilderness?

HUMILITY

The Lord wants justice, kindness, and humility. Amen. And be blessed. Gloria.

Discussion
Letting go of pride
Proverbs 22:4

HOLY GHOST

The Holy Ghost is the Spirit of God, our Father, whose son's name is Jesus Christ. We must know that he has all the power. Did you know that he is the feeling inside that gives you faith? The Holy Ghost has the power to heal in your living and the Holy Spirit. Trust in him and let the Holy Ghost bear fruit. Peace be still with the Holy Ghost.

THANKSGIVING

Wait on the Lord and be grateful. Thank him for all the good things he has done.

Have mercy on me. Lead me and carry me to the promised land.

God is still giving out blessings. Thanks be to God for the many gifts. Amen. Happy Thanksgiving.

Discussion

VETERANS DAY

Happy Veterans Day! Thanks be to God.

Thank you for your services and your continued dedication to our country, honoring American Veterans Day. The cessation of hostilities is commemorated in many countries as fought by American people of all colors. Amen. Gloria.

Discussion
Psalm 23:1–14

Happy Father's Day

Happy Father's Day to all men! You are a blessing. I am grateful to know there is a God who is the receiver of such an important celebration. I am blessed and gracious to have known my father, who lives in my Father's house, where there is a spirit.

Happy Father's Day. Amen.

HAPPY MEMORIAL DAY

Happy Memorial Day! Let us honor our heroes in memory today. Let us reflect on the lost who served, as men and women who gave their lives away. Let us include the Civil War and World War II veterans and all other members of the military branches. Let us count our blessings today and stand proudly.

Sometimes, death leaves us with heartache, but God knows what is best for us. On this day, Happy Memorial Day! Go in God's spirit. I pray, amen.

HAVE FAITH IN PRAYER

Faith in prayer: I give my heart to peace, and in the spirit of love, keep on praying. Amen.

Discussion
1 Corinthians 15:58

LET US HAVE THE LIGHT

Let there be light after death through God's grace. Amen.

Discussion
Light after death
John 1:4

THE DESIRES OF GOD

The desires of God are the flesh, and who is against the spirit? The desires of the spirit are real and are against the flesh, and the flesh can be opposed to each other. To keep our faith is the answer to the desires of God. How does God become the flesh, but the flesh is God's spirit? Amen.

Discussion
Why is God becoming flesh?

AMAZING

What an amazing God! What is your name? Praise the Lord! Amen.

Reflection

My spiritual reflection on God's glory and the righteous is that I shout out for joy in my circumstances. Amen.

Understand

Understand that God gives us the spirit, but sometimes our spirit goes dry! It needs a little touch from Jesus. Amen.

Discussions
Why is the spirit dry?

WHAT A GLORIOUS DAY

"This is a glorious day in Christ the Lord," called David. Amen.

SPREAD THE WORD

Go and spread the word. Peace be with you! Amen.

LEANING ON THE LORD

Holy! Holy God of all, in the spirit of God! The world looks new because of the new fishermen! "When I come out of the wilderness, I am leaning on the Lord." Thanks be to God on this holy day. Amen.

GOD HEARS MY PRAYERS

God is here for those who are spiritually discerning all things, but I am resolved to make a change in the divine spirit's strength and the wisdom and love of God and the people of God's unchanging hand. Amen.

Discussions
Unchanging hand
Romans 8:35

HOPE WITH EXPECTATION

The expectation of hope is God's word and has the power to lead to him. You are in the hands of Jesus, who has the power to pray and love. If you are sick, he will heal you, especially if you are in a time of faith through healing in the positive outcome and respective circumstances we call hope. Amen.

Discussions
Hope is God.
Power
Luke 18:35–43
Romans 15:13

HOLD ON TO GOD'S HAND

Hold on to God's changing hands because he is a healer. No evil can come before him because God is here. My chain has been broken. Do not fear. I shall follow him all the days of my life. Amen.

MANIFESTING THE SPIRIT

Manifesting the spirit: Who is the kingdom of God? Is he the power of God and the Spirit of God? How do you experience or express your divinity on earth through the power of manifesting in God's kingdom? Hallelujah. Amen.

Discussion
How to manifest the spirit?

LORD, I AM TIRED

I am tired of weeping, Lord. Too many are dying in the street with a gun held over them. Lord, I am tired of fighting for freedom. Lord, I ask you to protect all of your children from violence. My emotions and physical body are hurting. Lord, help your children to pray more. Please help me to teach the way so I can stop weeping. I can say this, Lord, that I am tired, and the weight I carry is a little heavy. Heal me from my tears. I am humble in my heart. Amen.

Discussion
John 16:33
Lamentations 3:22–23

POWER IN THE VALLEY

Who has the power? It is God in the valley who carries my heavy burdens. I am gracious because I sit in the middle of the valley. The power of the Holy Spirit deserves my life's gifts. I am the granddaughter of the prayer, so that the joy may completely dissolve as I give myself to God, with the balance of God's power in the valley. Amen.

BLACK WOMEN ARE PRAYING

Happy Mother's Day to all black women who are always praying. Indeed, they are special. They know what is going on in the world. Black mothers are always praying very silently.

Observe the manner in which black women care for their children. Despite the violence in this world, they continue to pour their endless love and support into their children. Hallelujah. Standing on the mountaintop, as the Lord lives, a mother's love is like God's love. On this day, I bless those black women who are praying and weeping as they know the love of God. May you continue to nurture our youth with your prayers. Amen.

Discussion:
Finally, be strong.
Ephesians 6:10–18
Isaiah 41–13

GOD KEEPS ON STRETCHING

God is always stretching and reaching out for you. YES! You're never alone. God is always with you. Why do we complain all the time? He reaches out more to us, and our reach is less. Even in these times, God sees us. Even when we don't see him, he sees us through the lens of his children. He sees our hearts. God has given the blessing. God's hand is reaching out for you. Don't turn away from it. Grab on to it! Be part of the church and grow stronger. He will increase our faith. Jesus knows us, and he will stretch our outcome in the world. Amen. Gloria.

EARTH HAS NO SORROW

Is there a sorrow on earth that cannot be fixed?
What has God equipped us with to mend these sorrows?
How has God revealed the truth and the life of humanity?
And how do joy and hope seek to keep the spirit alive? Amen.

Original

The earth has no sorrow that can't be fixed. What has God equipped us with, and how has God revealed the truth and the life? Joy seeks to understand how hope keeps the spirit alive.

Discussion
Isaiah 35:10
My trust in God

I am truly blessed and honored to know God for myself and trust in him. He will lead me in the right direction and to the Holy Spirit. Why should I not be afraid of God? The Holy Spirit is the truth of my life, and remember, whose faith should I follow and trust! Trust God. But take the yoke and divine. God has ordered your step but, he orders your faith and stump. Amen.

GOD SETS THE TONE

God sets the tone for Christ by lifting his eyes to heaven, so the people will follow. He states that the door is open.

Dear Lord, keep standing over me and giving me strength just like Father. For an hour, come glorify me in your name and set the tone. Amen.

TRUST GOD TRULY

I am blessed and honored to know and trust God. He will lead me into the Holy Spirit. The Holy Spirit is the truth of my life, and remember, whose faith should I follow and trust! God takes the youth and the divine. Why should I not fear God? Amen.

TROUBLE DOES NOT LAST ALWAYS

Dear God, I know your eyes are always on me. My trouble won't last. I am down and out, but I trust that you will provide me with the help I need. Holy Spirit, come here. I need you to place your hands around me with the strength of your body, which will give me hope and trust that my trouble does not always last.

God is in control. Amen.

Heavenly Father

Heavenly Father, may my hope be built on nothing less than Jesus's blood and his righteousness. Help me, as a Christian, to always be mindful of putting my hope in anything that is unfruitful other than you and your unfailing love.

Lord Jesus, fill me continually with your wisdom and power. In times of testing and trouble, may the eyes of my spirit see beyond my temporal circumstances and stay focused on that which is eternal. Thank you, Father, that you never change and that you are working all things out for my good. Amen.

—Mrs. Valerie Blunt

A PRAYER FOR MY MOTHER

"As a mother comforts her child, so will I comfort you" (Isaiah 66:13).

Heavenly Father, thank you for the gift of my mother. Thank you for all the years I enjoyed being with her. I am grateful to you when she stood with me through the good times and the bad times. I cherish the memories of times of joy and times of sorrow. As she is now at rest with you, I thank you for the hope of a future in your presence that we will share together. Now may you, the Lord of Peace, give me peace at all times and in every way. Through Jesus Christ, our Lord, amen.

—Mrs. Mary Minnis

BE JOYFUL

Have a hopeful life filled with joy. "Be joyful in hope, patient in afflictions, [and] faithful in prayer" (Romans 12:12).

Lord, I thank you for giving me hope. I don't know what my life would be like without you. I don't know what my future holds, but you give me hope and joy even while I wait—even when I don't understand. Please help me to have a positive attitude and live with a mindset of patience and courage as you let your will be done in my life. Help me remain faithful in prayer, Lord, fully relying on you. In the precious name of Jesus Christ, our Lord, amen.

—Mrs. Mary Minnis

ACKNOWLEDGMENTS

Edeme, Therese Elong-Manguith, editor
Wray, Dailyn Amandla, editor
West Charles, drawing artist
Betty Willis
Mary Minnis
Imogen Zachery
Valerie Blunt
Anika Pettus

ABOUT THE AUTHOR

Gloria Graham wrote this from the spirit who provided the words to her to just help somebody.

Everything will be fine because the Lord will provide. She is living for the Lord and knows that when she was sick, he was there, giving her what she needed. Life comes with a journey. This is her story.

* 9 7 9 8 8 9 0 6 1 3 5 5 4 *